FAR-OUT GUIDE TO
ASTEROIDS and COMETS

FAR-OUT GUIDE
to the
SOLAR SYSTEM

Mary Kay Carson

Bailey Books
an imprint of
Enslow Publishers, Inc.
40 Industrial Road
Box 398
Berkeley Heights, NJ 07922
USA
http://www.enslow.com

For Clayton Blaze Hammons

Bailey Books, an imprint of Enslow Publishers, Inc.

Library of Congress Cataloging-in-Publication Data

Carson, Mary Kay.
     Far-out guide to asteroids and comets / Mary Kay Carson.
        p. cm. — (Far-out guide to the solar system)
     Summary: "Presents information about asteroids and comets, including fast facts, history, and technology used to study them"—Provided by publisher.
     Includes bibliographical references and index.
     ISBN 978-0-7660-3188-3 (Library Ed.)
     ISBN 978-1-59845-191-7 (Paperback Ed.)
     1. Asteroid—Juvenile literature. 2. Comets—Juvenile literature. 3. Solar system—Juvenile literature.
  I. Title.
     QB651.C37 2011
     523.44—dc22

                  2009006484

Printed in China

052010 Leo Paper Group, Heshan City, Guangdong, China

10 9 8 7 6 5 4 3 2 1

Image credits: Armagh Observatory, p. 13; D. Roddy (U.S. Geological Survey), Lunar and Planetary Institute, p. 10; Don Davis/NASA, p. 9; ESA - AOES Medialab, pp. 1, 17, 24; ESA, image by AOES Medialab, p. 37; ESA-Service Optique CSG, p. 38; European Space Agency, p. 19 (comet); Lunar and Planetary Institute, p. 11; NASA, pp. 29, 32; NASA, ESA, and A. Feild (STScI), pp. 6 (top), 40; NASA/Caltech, p. 4; NASA/JPL, pp. 15 (bottom), 26 (right), 30, 33, 34 (left), 39, 41; NASA/JPL/JAXA, p. 14; NASA/JPL/USGS, p. 19 (asteroid); NASA/JPL-Caltech, pp. 3, 31; NASA/JPL-Caltech/University of Washington, p. 34 (right); NASA/UH/IA, p. 15 (top); Shutterstock, p. 25; T. Rector (University of Alaska Anchorage), Z. Levay and L.Frattare (Space Telescope Science Institute) and National Optical Astronomy Observatory/Association of Universities for Research in Astronomy/National Science Foundation, p. 26 (left); Tom Uhlman, p. 6 (bottom).

Cover image: Don Davis/NASA (asteroid illustration); European Space Agency (comet); Shutterstock (starfield).

CONTENTS

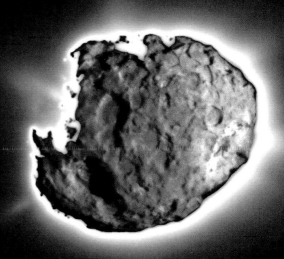

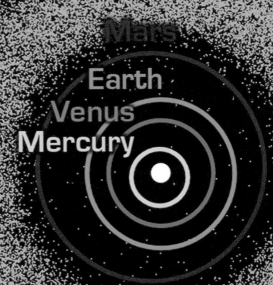

Jupiter

Mars

Earth
Venus
Mercury

Asteroid belt

INTRODUCTION

A chunky cloud swirled around our new Sun 4.5 billion years ago. The cloud of gas, dust, ice, and rock were leftovers from the Sun's birth. Most of the early solar system scraps bumped and clumped into big balls. They grew into planets and moons. But some of those ancient leftover chunks of rock and ice are still around. We call them comets and asteroids. You will learn lots more far-out facts about them in this book. Just keep reading!

MINIATURE WORLDS, BIG DISCOVERIES

Our solar system is home to millions of hunks of rock and metal, called asteroids. Most travel around, or orbit, the Sun in the asteroid belt between Mars and Jupiter. But some asteroids travel paths that go elsewhere—including near Earth.

THE asteroid belt is an area of space between Mars and Jupiter. It is 180 million kilometers (112 million miles) wide. The asteroids there never clumped into a planet. Why not? Jupiter's powerful pull of gravity prevented it.

ASTEROIDS come in many shapes and sizes. They range from boulder-sized to about one-fourth of our Moon's width. These four asteroid photographs are labeled with their widths.

Gaspra
(12 mi)

Eros
(21 mi)

Ida
(36 mi)

Vesta
(329 mi)

A comet looks like a fuzzy star with a streaky tail. This is comet Hale-Bopp. It shined in the night sky in 1997.

Beyond the planets are many billions of comets. Comets are icy hunks of frozen rock and dust. All comets orbit the Sun along long oval-shaped paths. When a comet nears the Sun, its ice warms and changes to gases. Its tail-like stream of gases and dust shines with reflected sunlight. While most comets orbit at the solar system's edge, others come nearer to Earth, like famous Halley's comet.

Comets and asteroids have changed little since the newly made solar system left them behind. Billions of years of storms, volcanoes, or other events changed the planets. But the stillness of space preserved comets and asteroids. They are full of clues about the young solar system. Scientists study comets and asteroids to find out how the solar system began, how it has changed, and how the planets and moons formed. They also keep an eye on asteroids and comets to make sure one does not hit Earth.

FAR-OUT FACT

WHAT ABOUT METEOROIDS?

What happens when an asteroid or comet breaks up? Meteoroids are made! Meteoroids are small bits of comets or asteroids that orbit the Sun. When a meteoroid enters Earth's atmosphere, it burns up. The light from the burning meteoroid you see in the sky is a meteor—also called a shooting star. If a piece of the meteoroid makes it all the way to the ground, the rock from space is a meteorite.

CHAPTER 1

TRACKING SPACE ROCKS

Asteroids and comets have been slamming into Earth since it formed. These crashes, called impacts, helped create the world we know. Comet crashes probably delivered some of early Earth's water. They also likely brought the chemicals needed for life. Sixty-five million years ago, an asteroid the size of Mount Everest crashed into southern Mexico. The explosion threw a lot of sky-darkening dust into the air. The climate cooled, the dinosaurs died out, and mammals—including humans—evolved to take their place. While asteroid and comet impacts shaped our world, a giant impact could tear civilization apart. Fortunately, scientists are on the lookout.

THIS illustration shows an asteroid slamming into young Earth. It is fifty times the size of the one that hit 65 million years ago.

BARRINGER METEORITE CRATER

This is Barringer Meteorite Crater, sometimes just called Meteor Crater. It is a giant, bowl-shaped hole in the northern desert of Arizona. The crater is nearly a mile wide and 1,200 meters (4,000 feet) in diameter. See the road leading to the visitor center at the top-right of the photograph? It gives you an idea of the crater's giant size. It is so deep that the Washington Monument could fit down inside it. Boulders the size of trucks lie around its rim. A meteoroid as wide as half a football field slammed into the ground about fifty thousand years ago, creating this large crater. The explosion was about 150 times as powerful as the atomic bombs of World War II.

INCOMING!

Small space rocks enter Earth's atmosphere all the time. As they fall, they burn up, creating streaks of light called meteors. Space rocks the size of a car or larger do not completely burn up. Speeding toward Earth many times faster than a bullet, they glow with fiery heat and slam into the ground with bomblike force. The exploding space rock creates an impact crater ten to twenty times bigger than itself.

An asteroid the size of a football field could destroy a large city. Rocks of this size hit Earth every thousand years or so. The most worrisome are the most rare—the really big asteroids. The asteroid that ended the dinosaurs was

EARTH has many craters left from asteroid, comet, and meteoroid impacts. This map shows where large impact craters have been found on land.

about ten kilometers (six miles) wide. An impact this big only happens every few million years on average. How can we know when a dangerous comet or asteroid is coming? That is the job of the NEO Program.

Most asteroids and comets orbit far from Earth. Those that do travel close to Earth are called near-Earth objects, or NEOs. The NEO Program finds, tracks, and studies these nearby objects. "It's our job to . . . make sure that none of these objects are getting dangerously close to the Earth," explained Don Yeomans. Yeomans is a comet and asteroid expert who worked on spacecraft missions to NEOs. (See *NEAR* and *Deep Impact* missions on the Asteroid and Comet Timeline of Exploration and Discovery on page 25.) Now he heads the NEO Program's team of scientists searching the skies with telescopes. "We discover these objects. We try and determine what they're made of, where they're going, and just how dangerous they might be," Yeomans explained.

FINDING NEOs

NEO scientists use telescopes on Earth to search for comets and asteroids. Cameras in the telescopes take pictures of the same section of the night sky over time. Any unknown objects seen gliding across the background of unmoving stars are investigated as possible **NEOs**. Starting in 2010, **NEO** hunters will have a new tool. The Canadian *Near Earth Object Surveillance Satellite* (*NEOSSat*) is the first space telescope designed to find **NEOs**. From space *NEOSSat* will have a clearer view of neighborhood asteroids and comets.

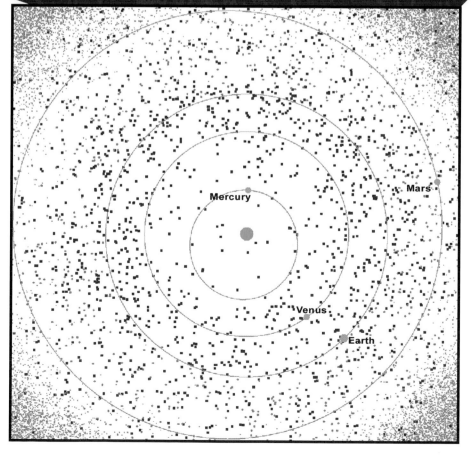

THE green dots on this map are asteroids or comets that do not come close to Earth. Yellow and red dots are near-Earth objects. Red dots are **NEOs** that cross Earth's orbit, and yellow dots are **NEOs** that come close to Earth but do not cross its orbit.

13

UNLUCKY ASTEROID

NEO Program scientists have discovered morethan 5,800 objects so far, 750 of which are more than one kilometer (0.6 miles) wide. About one thousand of the NEOs could cause trouble for Earth someday. One NEO everyone is watching is asteroid Apophis. "It's an object about

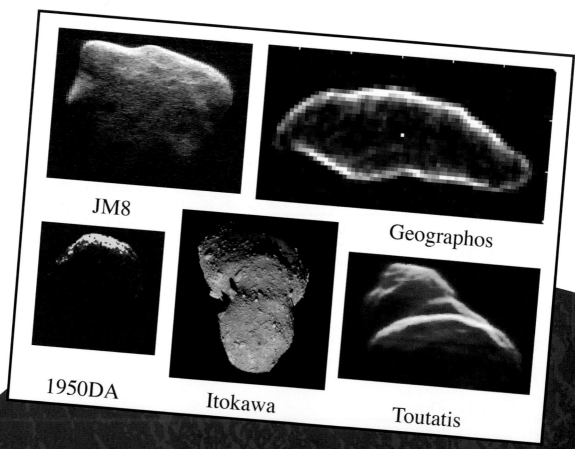

JM8

Geographos

1950DA

Itokawa

Toutatis

THESE asteroids are five of the NEOs listed as possible problems for Earth. Radar telescopes have studied asteroid JM8 in detail. Asteroid Geographos is more than five kilometers (three miles) long. Asteroid 1950DA was one of the first NEOs ever found, sixty years ago. Asteroid Itokawa is small at 550 meters (1,804 feet) across, but Japanese space probe *Hayabusa* visited it in 2005. Asteroid Toutatis is covered in big craters of its own.

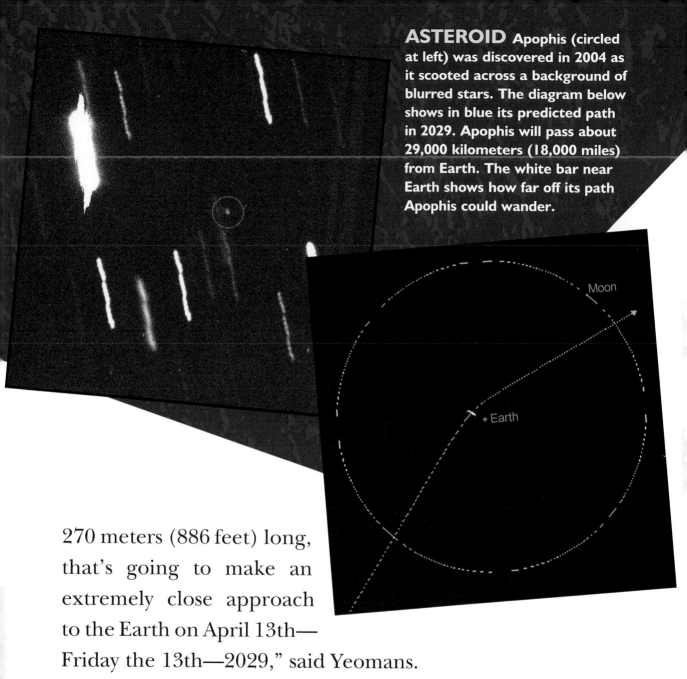

Moon

Earth

270 meters (886 feet) long, that's going to make an extremely close approach to the Earth on April 13th— Friday the 13th—2029," said Yeomans.

When the 20-million-ton asteroid Apophis was first discovered, scientists thought it had a good chance of hitting Earth in 2029. A land impact that size could destroy a country the size of England. An ocean impact could make waves big enough to wash away much of California's coast. But after studying Apophis more, the asteroid became less of a worry. "It's much like predicting a hurricane," explained Yeomans. "When it's first spotted, you don't know where it's going to hit. As you get more and more information on its track, you can predict where it's going to go."

Fortunately, the updated information on Apophis's path has it missing Earth. "Apophis is not really a threat," Yeomans said. While the asteroid will not hit Earth, Apophis will pass close enough in 2029 to see with the naked eye over Europe and North America. "It's going to be quite a sight," says Yeomans. Mark your calendar!

NUDGING AWAY DOOM

What can be done if—or when—scientists do spot an NEO that is on a crash course with our planet? Sending a missile to blow it up would likely make things worse. Instead of one asteroid coming toward Earth, we could end up with many still-dangerous space rocks on the way. A safer way would be to change its speed or course long

HOW TO MOVE AN NEO

Scientists want to be able to move an **NEO** that's on its way toward Earth so it does not impact us. Just a small push could change its future path and keep us safe. But how do you give an asteroid a shove? One idea is to send a spacecraft that would somehow pull, push, or shoot an asteroid-shoving projectile at the **NEO**. Another idea is to make the **NEO** move by heating it up with lasers or wrapping it with material that soaks up sunlight.

ONE NEO-moving robotic spacecraft being designed is called *Don Quijote*. Once at the asteroid or comet, it sends a projectile to crash into the **NEO**, shoving it off course.

before it reaches us. "[S]low it down, or speed it up, so that in twenty or thirty years, when it was predicted to hit the Earth, it would be [changed] just enough that it would miss the Earth," said Yeomans. Scientists and engineers have some ideas on how to nudge an NEO out of the way. How would you do it?

Whatever plan is picked, scientists and engineers will need time to put it into action. Finding an NEO that is going to crash into Earth tomorrow does not help anyone. We need to know about troublesome NEOs long before they get here. "An object like Apophis is just the tip of the iceberg," said Yeomans. "[M]y concern is the tens of thousands of these objects that we haven't yet discovered, and that could take us by surprise if we don't discover them." That is why the NEO hunters keep searching, tracking, and studying what is out there. "We don't let down our guard, not even for a day," said Yeomans.

ASTEROIDS
AT A GLANCE

Diameter: Up to 940 kilometers (564 miles)

Position: Most are located between Mars and Jupiter.

Average Distance of the Asteroid Belt From the Sun:
405 million kilometers (250 million miles)

Day Length of Larger Asteroids: Five to ten hours

Year Length (Time to Orbit the Sun): Approximately 600 to 2,000 Earth days

Color: Reddish or dark gray

Atmosphere: None

Surface: Rock

Moons: Some have at least one.

Rings: None (so far)

COMETS
AT A GLANCE

Diameter of Nucleus: Up to sixteen kilometers (ten miles)

Year Length (Time to Orbit the Sun): Up to 30 million Earth years

Atmosphere (Coma): Ammonia, carbon dioxide, carbon monoxide, and methane

Surface: Ice with rock and dust

Moons: None (so far)

Rings: None

ASTEROIDS

Asteroid Fast Facts

★ Asteroids are large rocks made of stone and metal orbiting the Sun.

★ Asteroids come in many shapes, and most are not round.

★ The mass of all the asteroids combined is less than that of the Moon.

★ There are more than ninety thousand identified asteroids.

★ Most of the solar system's millions of asteroids are between Mars and Jupiter.

★ Asteroids are leftovers from when the solar system formed about 4.5 billion years ago.

★ When Jupiter formed 4.5 billion years ago, its gravity likely stopped the asteroids in the asteroid belt from clumping together into their own planet.

★ Asteroids can get knocked or pulled out of their orbit and hit planets, including Earth.

★ Mars's small moons, Phobos and Deimos, are captured asteroids, as are some of the moons of the gas giant planets.

★ An asteroid that hit Earth 65 million years ago likely led to the extinction of the dinosaurs.

★ An asteroid crashing into Earth travels at 48,000 to 64,000 kilometers (30,000 to 40,000 miles) per hour.

★ Meteoroids are small, broken-up bits of asteroids or comets in space.

★ A meteor, or shooting star, is a meteoroid burning up in the atmosphere.

★ Meteorites are the rocky remains of meteoroids found on Earth.

★ At least two dozen asteroids have their own moons. Scientists call these binary asteroids.

★ Vesta is the brightest asteroid and the only one sometimes seen without a telescope.

★ Ceres is the biggest asteroid and is also a dwarf planet.

Asteroid Mission Fast Facts

★ Jupiter orbiter *Galileo* was the first space probe to see an asteroid, Gaspra, up close in 1991. It also discovered the first moon (Dactyl) of an asteroid (Ida) in 1993.

★ The first space probe to land on an asteroid was *Near Earth Asteroid Rendezvous* (*NEAR*). It orbited and landed on asteroid Eros in 2001.

★ Japanese space probe *Hayabusa* landed on asteroid Itokawa in 2005 and attempted to collect pieces of it. If the capsule reaches Earth in 2010 and contains some of Itokawa, *Hayabusa* will be the first asteroid sample-return mission.

COMETS

Comet Fast Facts

★ Comets are "dirty snowballs" chunks of ice, rock, and gases that orbit the Sun.

★ Comets have three main parts: nucleus, coma, and tail.

★ A comet nucleus is a small solid ball of ice and dust covered in a crust of dirt and gravel.

★ The ice in a comet is mostly frozen water but can also include frozen ammonia, carbon dioxide, carbon monoxide, and methane.

★ The coma is the comet's cloudy atmosphere of dust and gases.

★ The tail is the stream of gases and dust flowing away from the Sun.

★ When a comet nears the Sun, the ice of the nucleus changes to gases and blows holes in the crust. The jets of gases and dust become its coma and tail.

★ The Sun's rays and solar wind blow the coma away from the comet, creating the comet's long, bright tail, which always points away from the Sun.

★ Sunlight reflecting off the coma and tail is what we see from Earth as a comet.

★ Comets are leftovers from when the solar system formed about 4.5 billion years ago.

★ Short-period comets take fewer than two hundred years to orbit the Sun. Most come from the Kuiper belt beyond the orbit of Neptune.

★ Long-period comets take from 200 to 300 million years to circle the Sun. Many long-period comets come from the Oort cloud, a region of icy objects a hundred thousand times farther away than the distance between Earth and the Sun.

★ The Oort cloud may be home to as many as a trillion comets.

★ Early Earth was hit by many comets, and some likely delivered water and life-creating chemicals.

Comet Mission Fast Facts

★ Five space probes from Japan, Russia, and Europe flew out to study Halley's comet in 1986.

★ Jupiter-studying space probe *Galileo* observed and photographed comet Shoemaker-Levy 9 as it broke up and crashed into Jupiter in 1994.

★ When the spacecraft *Deep Impact* sent its impactor into comet Tempel 1 in 2005, it blew out a crater as big as a football field and as deep as a seven-story building.

★ The *Stardust* space probe was the first sample return from a body in deep space beyond the Moon.

Asteroid and Comet Timeline
of Exploration and Discovery

(Years given for successful spacecraft missions are when they explored the asteroid or comet. This might be different from the launch year.)

Prehistory—Humans observe comets' sudden appearances in the night sky.

1059 B.C.—Chinese astrologer records a comet sighting.

1705—Edmond Halley correctly predicts that a comet will reappear in 1758.

1801—Giuseppe Piazzi is the first to discover an asteroid, Ceres.

1802 to 1805—Heinrich Olbers discovers asteroids Pallas and Vesta.

1866—Giovanni Schiaparelli suggests that meteor showers are caused by Earth passing through the orbit of a comet.

1884 to 1885—Johann Palisa discovers asteroids Ida and Mathilde.

1898—Gustav Witt discovers asteroid Eros.

1908—Large meteoroid explodes over Tunguska, Russia, destroying 2,072 square kilometers (800 square miles) of forest.

1950—Jan Oort suggests that some comets come from a faraway cloud of icy chunks.

1951—Gerard Kuiper suggests that some comets come from a belt of icy objects beyond Pluto.

1985—*ICE* is the first spacecraft to visit a comet, Giacobini-Zinner.

1986—*Vega 1*, *Vega 2*, *Sakigake*, *Suisei*, and *Giotto* fly by and study Halley's comet.

1994—*Hubble Space Telescope* photographs comet Shoemaker-Levy 9's impact with Jupiter.

1997—*Near Earth Asteroid Rendezvous (NEAR)* space probe flies by asteroid Mathilde.

1999—*Deep Space 1 (DS1)* probe flies by asteroid Braille.

2000 to 2001—*NEAR* orbits asteroid Eros and then lands on it.

2001—*DS1* probe flies by comet Borrelly.

2005—*Deep Impact* spacecraft sends an impactor probe into comet Tempel 1. Space probe *Hayabusa* lands on asteroid Itokawa and attempts to collect samples.

2006—*Stardust* delivers collected comet tail particles from comet Wild 2 to Earth.

2010—*Hayabusa* to deliver its capsule to Earth.

2011—*Stardust* to study comet Tempel 1 and the crater left by *Deep Impact*. Orbiter *Dawn* to arrive at asteroid Vesta.

2014—Space probe *Rosetta* to become the first to land on a comet.

2015—*Dawn* to arrive at asteroid Ceres.

2029—Asteroid Apophis to make a close pass by Earth.

2061—Halley's comet to appear in the night sky.

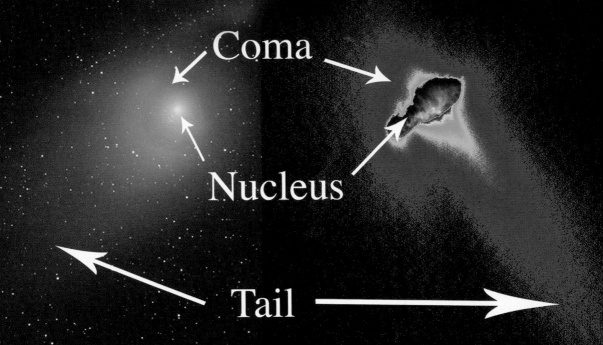

Coma

Nucleus

Tail

YOU can see the nucleus, cloud-like coma, and tail in these comet images. The left picture is comet **NEAT** taken through a telescope. The image of comet Borrelly on the right was taken by the *Deep Space 1* spacecraft. The added colors highlight the jets of gases and dust coming off the nucleus.

FAR-OUT FACT

HALLEY'S COMET

The English astronomer Edmond Halley studied the paths of comets in the late 1600s. He showed that comets orbit the Sun. Halley also predicted that the comet seen in 1682 would be back in 1758. When the comet returned on schedule, it earned Halley's name. Since then, Halley's comet has become famous. Its short orbit brings the easy-to-see comet past Earth every seventy-six years or so. In 1986 five spacecraft flew out to meet Halley's comet and study it (see page 25). Make sure to catch Halley's comet when it comes back in 2061.

CHAPTER 2

COMETS UP CLOSE

A comet is a sight to remember! People have carefully recorded comet sightings since ancient times. These days, spacecraft are giving us a closer look at comets. The new discoveries being made by space probes are rewriting the book on these icy scraps from the early solar system.

A comet is an icy object that orbits the Sun. It has three main parts: nucleus, coma, and tail. The nucleus is kind of like a big, dirt-covered, lumpy snowball. It is made of frozen water and other ices covered in a dark crust of dirt and gravel. When a comet travels near the Sun, the heat melts the ice and changes some of it into gas. Jets of gases and dust burst through holes in the nucleus's crust and create a cloud called a coma.

Solar wind and rays push the cloudy coma away from the Sun, like a fan blows away smoke. This creates a long tail of gases and dust. It is a comet's coma and tail that glow. Their gases and dust reflect light and shine. What exact ingredients make up the dust in a comet's tail? Peter Tsou is a scientist on a space probe mission that aims to find out. *Stardust* brought comet pieces to Earth. "Getting a sample from a comet but not landing on it is probably the best chance we have of discovering what the solar system was like 4.5 billion years ago," said Tsou.

FAR-OUT FACT

THE LONG AND SHORT OF COMETS

A short-period comet generally takes fewer than two hundred years to orbit the Sun. Short-period comets mostly come from the Kuiper belt, the area of icy stuff (including Pluto and Eris) beyond Neptune. Long-period comets generally make two-hundred-year or longer journeys around the Sun. Many of them come from the much farther away Oort cloud, a region of icy objects about a thousand times farther away from the Sun than Pluto. Gravity from the outer planets or passing stars can pull distant icy bodies closer to the Sun and turn them into comets.

STARDUST scientist Peter Tsou shows reporters a collector like the one on board the space probe. Tsou invented *Stardust*'s dust-capturing technique.

Tiny samples from a di...

CATCH A COMET'S TAIL

Stardust is the first space probe to fly through a comet's tail, collect some of its dust, and deliver it back to Earth. A comet dust collector was attached to the spacecraft. The collector looks like an oddly shaped ice-cube tray. Scientists filled the collector with special dust-capturing gel. *Stardust* flew within 240 kilometers (149 miles) of comet Wild 2. First, it photographed some stunning scenery! The pictures showed a solid object covered in craters and towers of rock. Comet Wild 2 is not simply a big, dirty snowball.

Next, it was time to collect comet dust. *Stardust* opened its capsule and held out the collector. The spacecraft safely flew through comet Wild 2's tail of fast-flying dust and gases. Luckily, none of the larger, pea-sized chunks hit the spacecraft. The gel inside the collector filled with tiny bits of comet tail dust. Then *Stardust* packed up its collector and headed home.

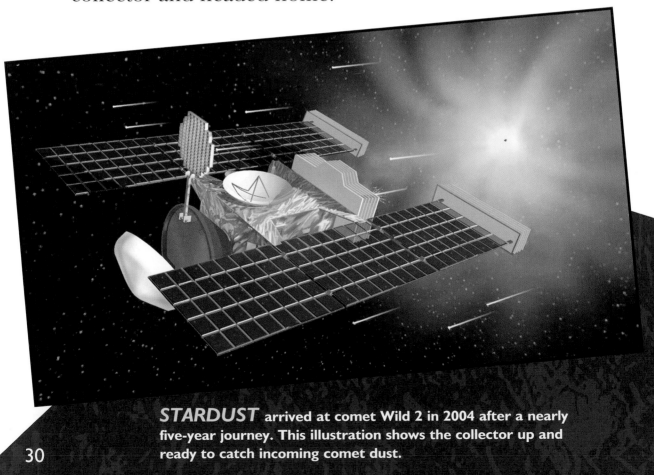

STARDUST arrived at comet Wild 2 in 2004 after a nearly five-year journey. This illustration shows the collector up and ready to catch incoming comet dust.

HOLDING ONTO THE PAST

After traveling for seven years and 3.2 billion miles, *Stardust* arrived back above Earth in 2006. Peter Tsou was one of the many nervous *Stardust* scientists. "I have been waiting twenty-five years for this time," Tsou told reporters. Fortunately, all went as planned. *Stardust* released its precious capsule of collected comet bits. It parachuted safely down to the Utah desert. Some of comet Wild 2 had arrived on Earth!

Stardust scientists popped open the capsule in the laboratory. Tsou knew right away that they had what they wanted. Millions of trapped comet dust bits had made tiny tracks in the gel, like pebble-pelted Jell-O. "This is the first time a human eye has seen comet dust," said Tsou. "[I]t may help us to find clues on how the solar system formed."

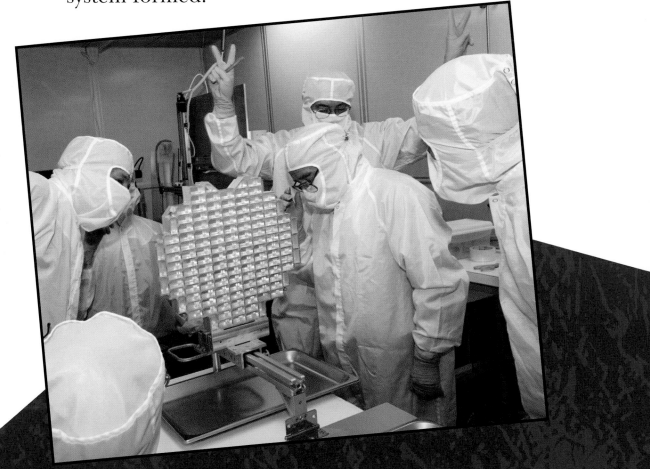

STARDUST scientists flash a V-for-victory sign when they take a first look at the comet dust collector. They wear special clean-room suits to keep from getting any Earth dust mixed in with the extraterrestrial comet dust.

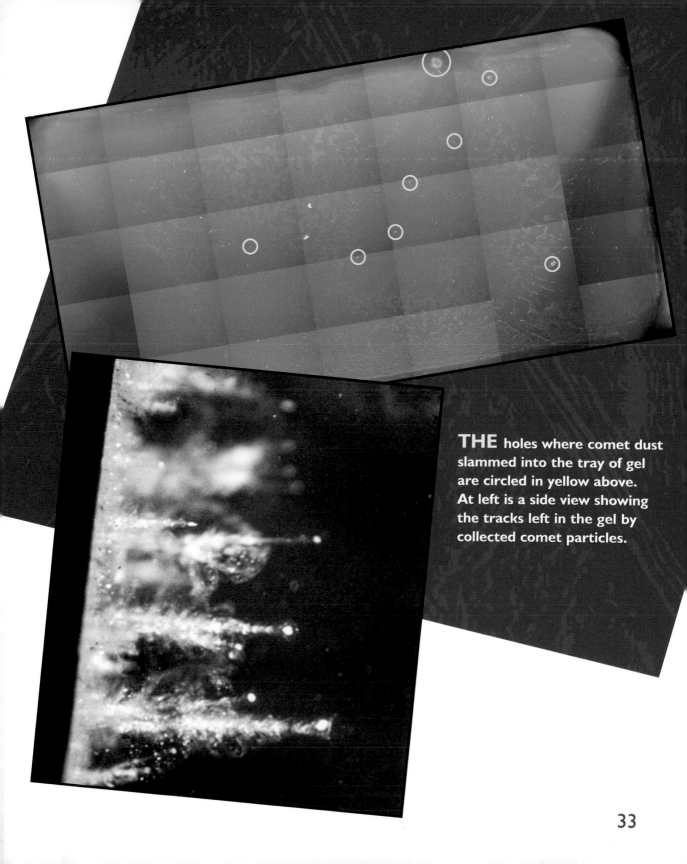

THE holes where comet dust slammed into the tray of gel are circled in yellow above. At left is a side view showing the tracks left in the gel by collected comet particles.

THESE are two magnified comet particles collected by *Stardust*. "Tiny samples from a distant comet open a giant window to our past," said Peter Tsou.

Scientists around the world have begun studying the *Stardust* comet dust. What are they finding? The dust contains at least one important building block needed for life. There are also some big surprises. Many of comet Wild 2's particles formed near our Sun when it was very young. So how did they get into comets out past the planets? "It seems we have much more to learn about the solar system," said Tsou. And more to learn about comets. Luckily, *Stardust* is still on the job. It is already on its way to meet up with another comet, Tempel 1, in 2011.

DEEP IMPACT

Deep Impact was a mission to study what is deep inside a comet—by blowing a hole in it. The space probe *Deep Impact* flew to comet Tempel 1 in 2005. When it got there, it sent a 370-kilogram (815-pound) copper impactor into the comet's nucleus. The explosion blew out more dust and less ice than expected. In fact, so much dust flew off the comet that *Deep Impact*'s cameras had a hard time getting a good view. Now that the dust has cleared, *Stardust* will be going back to check out the crater in 2011.

METEOR SHOWERS

A comet bright enough to be seen in the night sky without a telescope is a rare event. You will probably hear about it in the news, if it happens. One comet-created sight you can count on seeing is a meteor shower. Meteor showers happen when Earth passes through the dust left by a comet. The dust and small rocks enter Earth's atmosphere, burning up with fiery light. Because comets orbit the Sun along a known pathway, meteor showers are predictable year after year. The Web sites listed on page 47 can help you find upcoming comets and meteor showers.

CHAPTER 3

WHAT'S NEXT FOR COMETS AND ASTEROIDS?

There is much more to learn about comets and asteroids. And a number of spacecraft are on their way to making new discoveries. Space probe *Deep Impact* will arrive at comet Hartley 2 in 2010. *Stardust* will reach comet Tempel 1 a year later. These two robotic explorers will study the comets as they fly by. But another is on its way to the first-ever comet landing.

The *Rosetta* spacecraft is now on a ten-year trip to Churyumov-Gerasimenko, a four-kilometer- (two-and-a-half-mile-) wide comet. Its mission is to study how comets change as they near the Sun.

THIS illustration shows the *Rosetta* lander on the surface of comet Churyumov-Gerasimenko in 2014. It will take pictures, study the comet's ices, and measure chemicals in its dirty crust.

"We have so many questions about the origins of the solar system and the origins of life and possibly life on other planets in our solar system," said *Rosetta* scientist Claudia Alexander. "Comets might provide key clues to some of these questions." Once *Rosetta* gets there in 2014, the spacecraft will send a separate lander down to

ENGINEERS work on getting *Rosetta*'s lander ready in 2002. It was later attached to the spacecraft, loaded into a rocket, and launched in 2004.

the comet's nucleus. Meanwhile, *Rosetta* will orbit comet Churyumov-Gerasimenko as it travels closer to the Sun, studying how the melting heat and solar rays change it.

MISSION TO MONSTER ASTEROIDS

Like comets, asteroids are time capsules. They hold the history of how our solar system formed. Asteroids very much like those still in the asteroid belt once clumped together to help make the planets 4.5 billion years ago. A spacecraft called *Dawn* will find out what these left-overs are made of. *Dawn* is now on its way to the asteroid belt. Its mission is to study two of its largest members up

VESTA and Ceres are two of the largest known asteroids. Ceres is by far the biggest. Ceres makes up more than one-fourth of all the mass in the asteroid belt.

THIS illustration shows *Dawn* circling asteroid Vesta in 2011. Instruments on the robotic spacecraft will study its rocks, craters, and gravity.

close—asteroids Vesta and Ceres. These big asteroids are like baby planets that stopped growing billions of years ago. They quit clumping with other asteroids when Jupiter formed.

Dawn's first stop will be Vesta in 2011. Vesta is a big chunk of dry rock and metal with a very hot past. The asteroid has marks of ancient lava flows and oceans of melted rock. "That's interesting—and a bit puzzling," said *Dawn* scientist Chris Russell. No one is sure how such a small world could have heated up so much.

Much more massive is *Dawn*'s second stop. Ceres is the asteroid belt's biggest member. It is so big that, like Pluto, it is called a dwarf planet. Ceres is also unlike most asteroids. It appears to have a thick layer of ice under its surface and might even have a very thin atmosphere. Scientists compare Ceres to some of the icy moons of

FAR-OUT FACT

CERES'S CHANGING STATUS

When the Italian astronomer Giuseppe Piazzi discovered Ceres in 1801, he called it a planet. But as other large, rocky worlds were found nearby, Ceres became the first of the newly discovered objects named asteroids. One hundred and fifty years later, Ceres was reclassified, along with Pluto, as a dwarf planet. Why? It fits the dwarf planet definition. Ceres orbits the Sun, it shares its orbit with other objects (asteroids), and its large size forces gravity to squash it into a round shape.

FAR-OUT FACT

SAMPLING AN ASTERIOD

In 2005 a Japanese spacecraft named *Hayabusa* touched down on asteroid Itokawa. It tried to grab a piece of the asteroid, but the robotic space probe was damaged during the mission. *Hayabusa* is trying to return its capsule to Earth in 2010. No one is sure whether or not anything is inside the capsule.

Saturn or Neptune. "Ceres is going to be a real surprise to us," said Russell. *Dawn* will photograph and study Ceres in 2015. The space probe's instruments will try to figure out what its surface is made of and also what lies underneath. Whatever it finds will help us better understand asteroids and comets—scraps left over from the solar system's birth.

★

Words to Know

asteroid—**A large rock that orbits the Sun.**

asteroid belt—**The region of space between Mars and Jupiter where most asteroids are found.**

binary system—**Two objects in space that orbit each other.**

comet—**A large chunk of ice, frozen gases, and dust that orbits the Sun.**

craters—**Bowl-shaped holes made by impact explosions, often from comet or asteroid crashes.**

dwarf planet—**A round space object that orbits the Sun and may share its orbit with other objects.**

gas giant—**A planet made of mostly gas and liquid and no land, including Jupiter, Saturn, Uranus, and Neptune.**

gravity—**The force of attraction between two or more bodies with mass.**

impact craters—**Craters left by an asteroid, a meteorite, or a comet crash.**

impactor—**Something that impacts, or crashes into, something else.**

lander—**A space probe that sets down on the surface of a planet or another object in space.**

mass—**The amount of matter in something.**

meteor—**A meteoroid burning up in the atmosphere; a shooting star.**

WORDS TO KNOW
★

meteorite—A meteoroid that fell from space and landed on Earth, or another space object.

meteoroid—A small chunk of space rock, often from crushed asteroids or broken-up comets.

meteor shower—Many meteors burning up in Earth's atmosphere.

methane—Natural gas, or a gas made of a combination of carbon and hydrogen.

orbit—The path followed by a planet, a moon, or an object in space around another object; to move around an object in space.

orbiter—A space probe that orbits a planet, a moon, or another object in space.

planet—A large, sphere-shaped object in space that is alone (except for its moons) in its orbit around a sun.

radar—A technology or device that uses reflected radio waves to find or map distant or unseen objects.

shooting star—A meteor.

solar wind—The constant stream of charged particles given off by the Sun.

space probe—A robotic spacecraft launched into space to collect information.

Sun—The star in the center of our solar system.

star—A large ball-shaped object in space made of hot gases that shines by its own light.

Find Out More and Get Updates

BOOKS

Bourgeois, Paulette. *The Jumbo Book of Space.* Toronto: Kids Can Press, 2007.

Carson, Mary Kay. *Exploring the Solar System: A History With 22 Activities.* Chicago: Chicago Review Press, 2008.

Kusky, Timothy. *Asteroids and Meteorites: Catastrophic Collisions with Earth.* New York: Facts On File, 2009.

Lopez, Delano. *Amazing Solar System Projects You Can Build Yourself.* White River Junction, Vt.: Nomad Press, 2008.

Miller, Ron. *Asteroids, Comets, and Meteors.* Minneapolis: Twenty-First Century Books, 2004.

Mist, Rosalind. *Could an Asteroid Hit the Earth? Asteroids, Comets, Meteors, and More.* Chicago: Heinemann, 2006.

FIND OUT MORE AND GET UPDATES
★

SOLAR SYSTEM WEB SITES

NASA. *StarChild.*
   http://starchild.gsfc.nasa.gov/

The Regents of the University of Michigan. *Windows to the Universe.*
   http://www.windows.ucar.edu/

ASTEROID AND COMET EXPLORATION WEB SITES

NASA/JPL. *Dawn Kids.*
   http://dawn.jpl.nasa.gov/dawnkids/

NASA/JPL. *Keeping an Eye on Space Rocks.*
   http://www.jpl.nasa.gov/multimedia/neo/

NASA/JPL. *Stardust.* "Kids and Parents Page."
   http://stardust.jpl.nasa.gov/classroom/kids.html

PLANET-WATCHING WEB SITES

Sky and Telescope. *Starmap.* "Comets."
   http://www.skyandtelescope.com/observing/objects/comets/

Space.com. *NightSky Sky Calendar.*
   http://www.space.com/spacewatch/sky_calendar.html

The University of Texas McDonald Observatory. *Stardate Online.*
   "Meteor Showers and Viewing Tips."
   http://stardate.org/nightsky/meteors/

Index